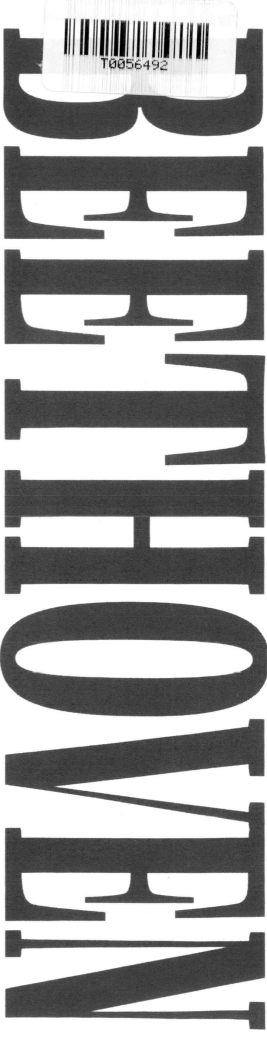

BEETHOVEN

Piano Trios
Nos. 8 and 11
"Kakadu Variations"

Emanuel Vardi
Violin

Alan Shulman
Cello

Edwin Hymovitz
Piano

MMO

3065

Music Minus One

3065

LUDWIG VAN BEETHOVEN
PIANO TRIOS
No. 8 in E-flat major, WoO38
No. 11 in G major ('Kakadu' Variations), op. 121a
for Piano, Violin, and Violoncello

Trio No. 8

for Violin, Violoncello and Piano

Op. Posth.

Ludwig van Beethoven
(1770 -1827)

MMO 3065

4

6

Trio No. 11
'Kakadu' Variations
for Violin, Violoncello and Piano
Opus 121a

Four quarter-note taps precede music

Ludwig van Beethoven
(1770 -1827)

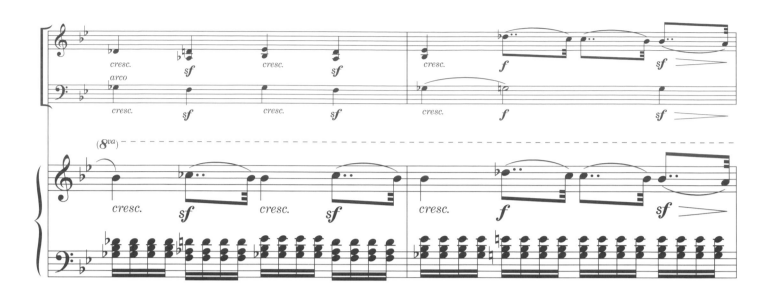

Var.I. (Piano solo)

Var. II.

Var.III.

dolce

cresc. _ _ _ _ _ _ _ _ _

Var.III.

p dolce

cresc. _ _ _ _ _ _ _ _

7 21 *Two quarter-note taps precede music*

Var. IV.

28

9 23 *Two quarter-note taps precede music*

Var. VI.

Var. VI.
leggiermente

34

MMO 3065

Var.IX.
Adagio espressivo.

Var.IX.
Adagio espressivo.

13 27 *Two dotted-quarter-note taps precede music*

Var. X.
Presto

Var. X.
Presto

46

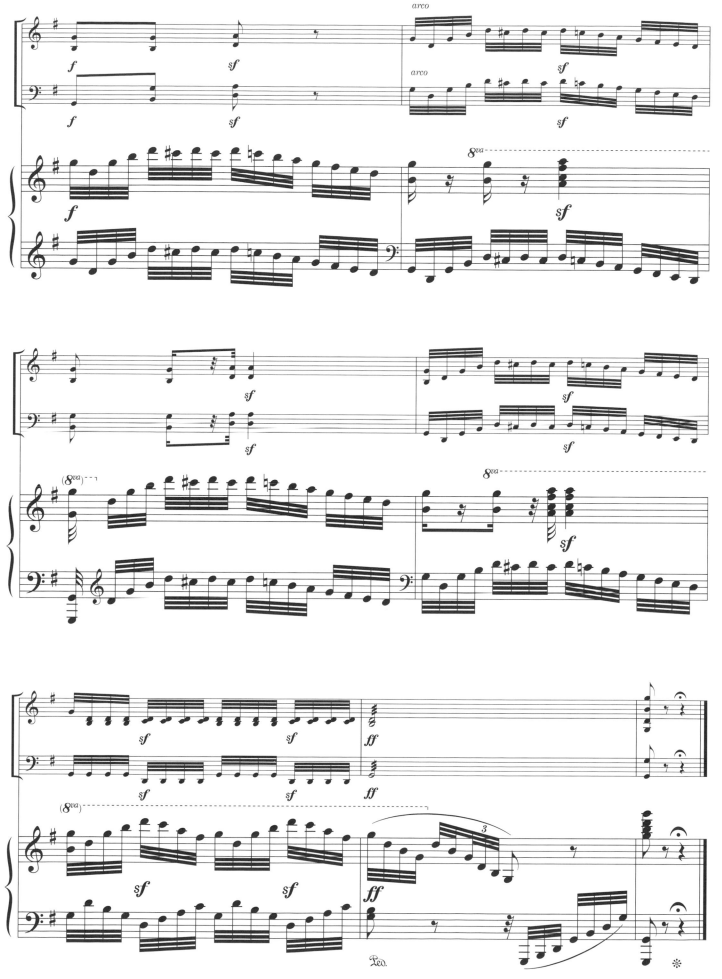

Engraving: Wieslaw Novak

MMO 3065

MUSIC MINUS ONE
50 Executive Boulevard
Elmsford, New York 10523-1325
800-669-7464 (U.S.)/914-592-1188 (International)

www.musicminusone.com
e-mail: mmogroup@musicminusone.com

Printed in Canada